A FIRST LOOK AT AMERICA'S PRESIDENTS

DWIGHT D. EISENHOWER

The 34th President

by Miriam Aronin

Consultant: David Greenberg, Professor of History
Rutgers University
New Brunswick, New Jersey

BEARPORT
PUBLISHING

New York, New York

Credits

Cover: Courtesy White House Historical Association; 4, © AP Photo; 5, Courtesy Eisenhower Library; 6, U.S. Army/Newscom; 7T, Courtesy Eisenhower Library; 7B, © Filimages/Shutterstock; 8, Courtesy Eisenhower Library; 9T, © Everett Historical/Shutterstock; 9B, © Philip Capper; 10, Courtesy Kansas State Historical Society; 11, Courtesy Eisenhower Library; 12, © AP Photo; 13, © AP Photo; 14, Courtesy collectorgene.com; 15, © Bettmann/Corbis; 16, Courtesy Eisenhower Library; 17, © John Lemmer/Dreamstime; 18, Carol Highsmith/Library of Congress; 19T, © Gehry Partners, LLP, 2015; 19B, Courtesy Eisenhower Library; 20T, Courtesy Eisenhower Library; 20BL, Courtesy Eisenhower Library; 20BR, Courtesy Eisenhower Library; 21T, IWM; 21B, © AP Photo; 21R, Carol Highsmith/Library of Congress; 22, © Americanspirit/Dreamstime; 23T, Courtesy collectorgene.com; 23M, Courtesy Eisenhower Library; 23B, © John Lemmer/Dreamstime; 24, Courtesy Kansas State Historical Society.

Publisher: Kenn Goin
Editor: Jessica Rudolph
Creative Director: Spencer Brinker
Production and photo research: Shoreline Publishing Group LLC

Library of Congress Cataloging-in-Publication Data

Names: Aronin, Miriam.
Title: Dwight D. Eisenhower / by Miriam Aronin.
Description: New York, New York : Bearport Publishing Company, 2016. |
   Series: First look at America's presidents | Includes bibliographical
   references and index. | Audience: 4-8._
Identifiers: LCCN 2015040016| ISBN 9781943553310 (library binding) | ISBN
   1943553319 (library binding)
Subjects: LCSH: Eisenhower, Dwight D. (Dwight David), 1890-1969—Juvenile
   literature. | Presidents—United States—Biography—Juvenile literature. |
   United States—Politics and government—1953-1961—Juvenile literature.
Classification: LCC E836 .A88 2016 | DDC 973.921092—dc23
LC record available at http://lccn.loc.gov/2015040016

For more information, write to Bearport Publishing Company, Inc., 45 West 21st Street, Suite 3B, New York, New York 10010. Printed in the United States of America.

10 9 8 7 6 5 4 3 2 1

CONTENTS

A Leader in War and Peace

Dwight D. Eisenhower spent his life serving his country. He fought in World War II and became a hero. Then he ran for president and worked toward peace. His efforts made our country better.

Eisenhower served in the U.S. Army for many years.

Eisenhower was sometimes called "Ike" for short.

Ike was the 34th president. He served from 1953 to 1961.

Growing Up in Kansas

Ike was born in 1890. He grew up in Kansas. Ike worked hard in school. His favorite subject was history. Yet he made time for fun. He loved to play baseball.

Ike

This picture shows young Ike with his family.

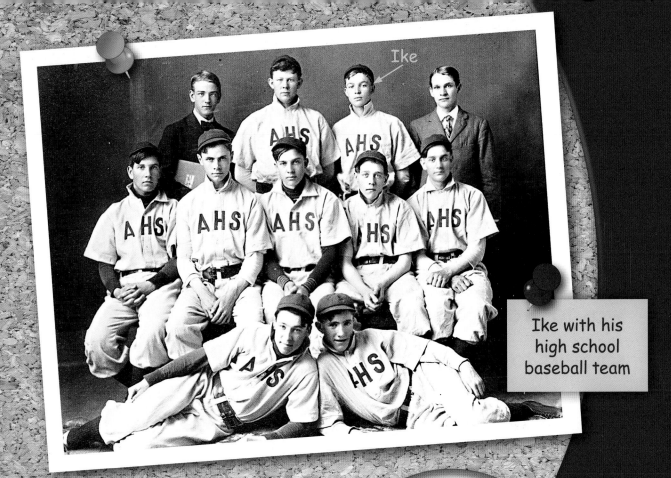

Ike

Ike with his high school baseball team

As a teen, Ike worked in a creamery. A creamery is a place that makes milk products.

Ike went to college in New York. There, he learned to lead soldiers. Later, he became a U.S. Army **officer**. One of Ike's jobs was to teach soldiers to fight using tanks.

Ike married Mamie Geneva Doud in 1916. He wore his army uniform at the wedding.

The United States and many other nations fought in World War I (1914–1918).

Ike was supposed to fig[ht] in World War I. Howeve[r,] the war in Europe ende[d] just before he left. Ike w[as] very disappointed.

Soldiers used tanks like this one in World War I.

The General Goes to War

In 1939, World War II started in Europe. The United States joined the war two years later. Ike was now a **general** in the army. His job was to plan big attacks on German troops. He planned the biggest attack of the war in 1944.

During World War II, Americans fought against Germany and other nations. Countries that fought with the United States, such as Britain, were called the Allies.

During the war, Ike designed a jacket for soldiers called the "Ike jacket."

Soldiers trusted General Eisenhower. He was a tough but caring leader.

A Big Day

The huge attack was called D-Day. More than 150,000 Allies took boats and planes from Britain to France. There, they fought German troops. The attack was a success. Germany soon **surrendered**.

On D-Day, about 4,000 warships carried Allied troops to beaches in France. It was one of the largest attacks in history.

American soldiers land on a beach in France.

Allies in Britain headed to France on D-Day, June 6, 1944.

North Sea

Great Britain

Atlantic Ocean

Germany

English Channel

France

E U R O P E

Thousands of American soldiers were wounded or killed during the D-Day attack.

America Likes Ike

After the war, Ike wanted to do more to help his country. He ran for president in 1952 and won the **election**. At the time, the United States was at war in Korea. As president, Ike worked hard to end the Korean War.

Ike had some of the first campaign ads on television. One ad was a cartoon made by Walt Disney!

A presidential campaign button

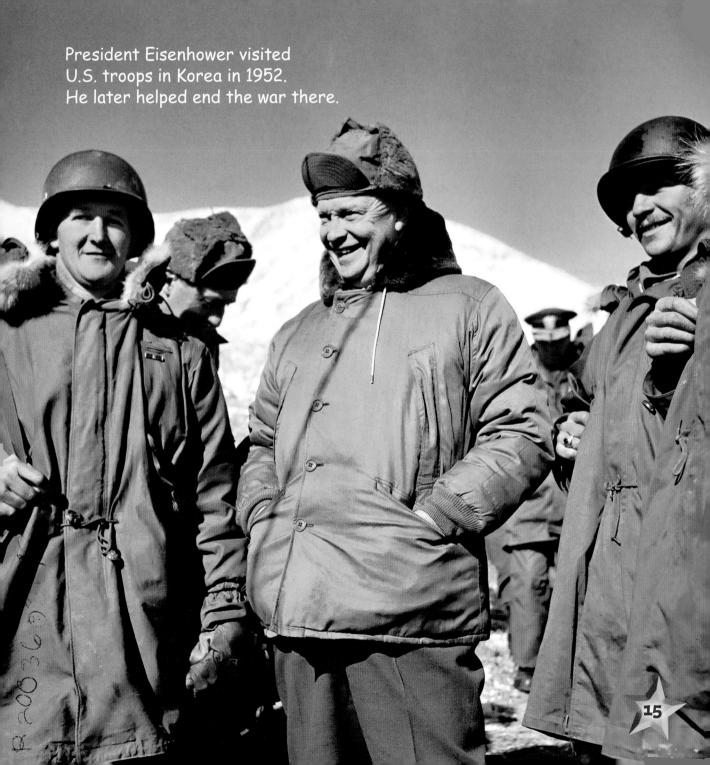

President Eisenhower visited
U.S. troops in Korea in 1952.
He later helped end the war there.

New Highways

In the 1950s, many parts of America had bad roads. In Europe, Ike had seen better roads that made driving safe and easy. He wanted America to have good roads, too. So, he helped create the **Interstate** Highway System.

In 1919, Ike made a cross-country trip. He saw rough dirt roads and broken bridges. The roads were so bad that the trip took two months.

Today, interst[ate]
highways stre[tch]
across the
entire count[ry.]

The nation kept growing while Ike was president. Alaska and Hawaii became states in 1959.

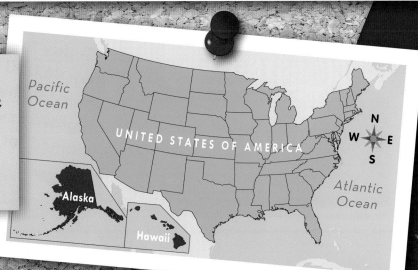

Remembering Eisenhower

Ike died in 1969. Today we remember him as a great leader. He helped the Allies win World War II. As president, he fought for peace. He helped our country become stronger.

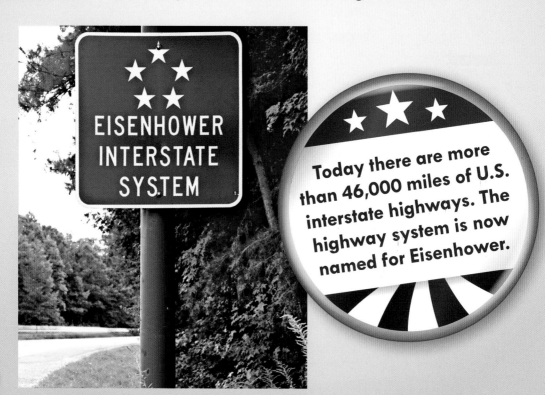

Today there are more than 46,000 miles of U.S. interstate highways. The highway system is now named for Eisenhower.

Ike

Ike worked well with other leaders. This helped him achieve his goals for America.

This is a model of the Eisenhower Memorial. It is scheduled to open in Washington, DC, in 2017. A memorial is a place that honors an important person or event.

THE TIDE HAS TURNED! THE FREE MEN OF THE WORLD ARE MARCHING TOGETHER TO VICTORY!

D-DAY ADDRESS TO TROOPS JUNE 6, 1944

Here are some
major events from
Dwight D. Eisenhower's life.

1890

Dwight D. Eisenhower
is born in Denison,
Texas. The next year,
his family moves to
Abilene, Kansas.

1911

Ike goes to a military
college called West Point.

1918

World War I ends.

1890 1900 1910 1920

Ike's childhood
home in Kansas

1916

Ike marries
Mamie Geneva
Doud.

1952
Ike is elected president.

1956
Ike is re-elected president. He signs a law to create the Interstate Highway System.

1941
The United States enters World War II. Ike becomes a general.

1930   1940   1950   1960   1970

1944
Ike plans the D-Day attack.

1953
Ike helps end the war in Korea.

1969
Ike dies in Washington, DC.

As president, Ike played golf and was very good at it. Today, he is in the Golf Hall of Fame.

"There is no end to America's forward road."

In 1955, President Eisenhower had a heart attack. He had to stay in the hospital for seven weeks. Luckily, he got better and ran for a second term as president.

"I hate war as only a soldier who has lived it can, only as one who has seen its brutality, . . . its stupidity."

GLOSSARY

campaign (kam-PAYN) an attempt to win a political office, such as president

election (i-LEK-shuhn) the selection of a person for office by voters

general (JEN-ur-uhl) the top officer in an army

interstate (IN-tur-stayt) connecting different states

officer (AWF-uh-sur) a leader in the military

surrendered (sur-REN-durd) gave up

Index

Read More

Alphin, Elaine Marie, and Arthur B. Alphin. *Dwight D. Eisenhower (History Maker Bios).* Minneapolis, MN: Lerner (2005).

Bird, Roy. *Little Ike: Dwight D. Eisenhower's Abilene Boyhood.* Stockton, KS: Rowe (2011).

Learn More Online

To learn more about Dwight D. Eisenhower, visit
www.bearportpublishing.com/AmericasPresidents

About the Author:
Miriam Aronin writes and edits books for kids. She lives in Chicago, Illinois.